SCRIPTURE
JOURNAL

THIRTY SCRIPTURE
PASSAGES ON

Love

:: CROSSWAY

WHEATON, ILLINOIS

You shall love your neighbor as yourself.

Leviticus 19:18

The LORD your God is God, the faithful God who keeps covenant and steadfast love with those who love him and keep his commandments, to a thousand generations.

Deuteronomy 7:9

Remember your mercy, O Lᴏʀᴅ, and your steadfast
love, for they have been from of old.

Psalm 25:6

....
....
....
....
....
....
....
....
....
....
....
....
....
....
....
....
....
....
....
....
....
....
....
....
....

I trust in the steadfast love of God forever and ever.

Psalm 52:8

I will sing of your strength; I will sing aloud of your steadfast love in the morning. For you have been to me a fortress and a refuge in the day of my distress.

Psalm 59:16

....

....

....

....

....

....

....

....

....

....

....

....

....

....

....

....

....

....

....

....

....

....

6

Oh give thanks to the Lord, for he is good, for his steadfast love endures forever!

Psalm 107:1-2

Let your steadfast love comfort me according to your promise.

Psalm 119:76

Hatred stirs up strife, but love covers all offenses.

Proverbs 10:12

A friend loves at all times, and a brother is born for adversity.

Proverbs 17:17

Set me as a seal upon your heart, as a seal upon your arm, for love is strong as death, jealousy is fierce as the grave. Its flashes are flashes of fire, the very flame of the LORD. Many waters cannot quench love, neither can floods drown it.

Song of Solomon 8:6-7

....

....

....

....

....

....

....

....

....

....

....

....

....

....

....

....

....

....

....

....

....

....

....

I have loved you with an everlasting love.

Jeremiah 31:3

....
....
....
....
....
....
....
....
....
....
....
....
....
....
....
....
....
....
....
....
....
....

The steadfast love of the LORD never ceases; his mercies never come to an end; they are new every morning; great is your faithfulness.

Lamentations 3:22–23

The LORD your God is in your midst, a mighty one who will
save; he will rejoice over you with gladness; he will quiet you
by his love; he will exult over you with loud singing.

Zephaniah 3:17

....

....

....

....

....

....

....

....

....

....

....

....

....

....

....

....

....

....

....

....

....

....

....

You shall love the Lord your God with all your heart and with all
your soul and with all your mind and with all your strength.

Mark 12:30

....
....
....
....
....
....
....
....
....
....
....
....
....
....
....
....
....
....
....
....
....
....
....
....
....
....
....
....

Love your enemies; do good to those who hate you.

Luke 6:27

....
....
....
....
....
....
....
....
....
....
....
....
....
....
....
....
....
....
....
....
....
....

For God so loved the world, that he gave his only Son, that whoever
believes in him should not perish but have eternal life.

John 3:16

....

....

....

....

....

....

....

....

....

....

....

....

....

....

....

....

....

....

....

....

....

....

....

A new commandment I give to you, that you love one another:
just as I have loved you, you also are to love one another.

John 13:34

....

....

....

....

....

....

....

....

....

....

....

....

....

....

....

....

....

....

....

....

....

Greater love has no one than this, that someone lay down his life for his friends.

John 15:13

....
....
....
....
....
....
....
....
....
....
....
....
....
....
....
....
....
....
....
....
....
....

God shows his love for us in that while we were still sinners, Christ died for us.

Romans 5:8

....

....

....

....

....

....

....

....

....

....

....

....

....

....

....

....

....

....

....

....

....

....

....

Let love be genuine. Abhor what is evil; hold fast to what
is good. Love one another with brotherly affection.

Romans 12:9–10

Love does no wrong to a neighbor; therefore love is the fulfilling of the law.

Romans 13:10

Love is patient and kind; love does not envy or boast; it is not arrogant or rude. It does not insist on its own way; it is not irritable or resentful; it does not rejoice at wrongdoing, but rejoices with the truth.

1 Corinthians 13:4–6

Love bears all things, believes all things, hopes all
things, endures all things. Love never ends.

1 Corinthians 13:7–8

....

....

....

....

....

....

....

....

....

....

....

....

....

....

....

....

....

....

....

....

....

So now faith, hope, and love abide, these three; but the greatest of these is love.

1 Corinthians 13:13

Let all that you do be done in love.

1 Corinthians 16:14

Put on love, which binds everything together in perfect harmony.

Colossians 3:14

....
....
....
....
....
....
....
....
....
....
....
....
....
....
....
....
....
....
....
....
....
....
....
....

Keep loving one another earnestly, since love covers a multitude of sins.

1 Peter 4:8

By this we know love, that he laid down his life for us, and
we ought to lay down our lives for the brothers.

1 John 3:16

....
....
....
....
....
....
....
....
....
....
....
....
....
....
....
....
....
....
....
....
....

Beloved, let us love one another, for love is from God, and whoever loves has been born of God and knows God. Anyone who does not love does not know God, because God is love.

1 John 4:7–8

....
....
....
....
....
....
....
....
....
....
....
....
....
....
....
....
....
....
....
....
....
....
....
....
....
....
....
....
....
....
....
....

There is no fear in love, but perfect love casts out fear.

1 John 4:18

ESV SCRIPTURE JOURNAL:
THIRTY SCRIPTURE PASSAGES ON LOVE

Copyright © 2016 by Crossway

ISBN: 978-1-4335-5323-3

Published by Crossway, 1300 Crescent Street, Wheaton, Illinois 60187

First printing 2016, Printed in China

Crossway is a publishing ministry of Good News Publishers.

RRDS	23	22	21	20	19	18	17	16
9	8	7	6	5	4	3	2	1